All are loved beyond measure

Taking Dictation:
Love Notes from God

Brenda Lycans

First Edition

Water Songs Publishing

Taking Dictation: Love Notes from God

Brenda Lycans
Water Songs Publishing
Post Office Box 224
Covington, KY 41011 USA
859.431.7740
info@watersongsonline.com

All rights reserved. No part of this book may be reproduced or transmitted in any form or by any means, electronic or mechanical, including photocopying, recording or by any information storage and retrieval system, without written permission from the author, except for the inclusion of brief quotations in a review.

Copyright © 2009 by Brenda Lycans

First Edition 2010

Brenda Lycans
Taking Dictation: Love Notes From God
First Edition ©2009
ISBN13: 978-0-615-36583-1
Self-publishing – United States
Brenda Lycans
Water Songs Publishing
Taking Dictation: Love Notes from God

Separation is an illusion

One

It begins with faith. You must be willing to trust to a higher power, something outside of yourself, and let go. Let go of the ideas we've all been raised with about knowledge; that we can actually say with any certainty that we really know anything.

Time and time again throughout the ages we have been proven wrong in what we 'know'. 500 years ago everyone 'knew' that the world was flat. 100 years ago everyone 'knew' that there wasn't anything invisible to our naked eye such as germs, or bacteria. In fact those physicians who suggested it were ridiculed and pushed out of the medical profession. But still they found that washing their hands between autopsies and births resulted in a higher rate of survival of both mothers and children. Millions died as a result of disease as rats and mice were viewed as an inconvenience rather than a health hazard, and open sewers ran through large cities. These experiences should have taught us not to put too much trust into what is known. But the ego holds a powerful place and insists that we know what is right (and wrong).

What we now assume we 'know' is coming into debate on many subjects, but still one hard and fast rule seems to remain locked in our minds. The idea that God is somehow far removed from us, untouchable; and unknowable. I can tell you, truly, this is not the case. God is such a slight shift in consciousness away that once there it becomes unimaginable that we haven't seen it all along. We, as a society, go through life without ever being taught this shift in awareness, without ever being taught to experience this amazing union. Once the shift is made it is actually difficult to remember where your consciousness could have existed before. Once this shift is made, life and the world begin to make sense. You begin to feel like you are part of something extraordinary and beautiful.

For me it began with an idea to make drinking glasses with Dr. Emoto's water crystals etched on them. I had seen a brief view of his work in the movie 'What the Bleep Do We Know?' and investigated further. He exposed water to words, froze drops, then watched and photographed them while thawing under a microscope. He found that water exposed to positive words form beautiful, structured crystals that rise out of the drops as they thaw. Water exposed to negative words not only do not form crystals, but thaw as disjointed bubbles, sometimes even off color, looking diseased. The idea presented was that water reflects what it is shown at a much deeper level than we thought (we 'knew'). I believe these crystals are the words interpreted in the language of water. As such, how wonderful I thought it would be to put them on glasses to drink from and have them convey these messages to the water in the drink and then on to our own water as we drink from them. Words (and their energy) like: Love & Gratitude, Peace, and Happiness could all be taken in with each sip, casually and effortlessly altering our own experience.

I contacted a local premier glass etching company who agreed to warehouse and ship for me as well as provide the etching. I contacted Dr. Emoto's company to see if they might consider allowing me to do this. They quickly granted me the rights. The Board of Commissioners in the city I live in gave me a business loan with acceptance and hope for the idea of it. I was amazed at how everything progressed. Then I was left with the question of how am I going to do the designs? The crystal images from micro-photography were blurry and uneven while the crystals were extraordinarily detailed. I tried computer software, but nothing I found could clear the images to something I could use. I had to draw them. I was very skeptical as to my abilities to do this, but I could find no other way. I sat down with a blank piece of paper and a printed image of the Love & Gratitude crystal. Actually, I sat down like this several times before anything was drawn, giving up and walking away. Finally, I put my faith in a higher power to get this done. I sat down and started drawing and it happened, the crystal began forming itself on the paper. As it did, I was filled with the feelings of love & gratitude. I drew eight crystals this way, each one forming itself with the feel of the words sweeping over me. Lines appeared that I couldn't see in the photos without straining my eyes. I was amazed. Somehow those drawings were channeled, I thought. I was very grateful and felt like I was doing something that the Universe approved of and helped with.

    As part of the licensing contract I went to study with Dr. Emoto. What a wonderful experience that was. I would never have imagined the possibility of being able to do that. During one session, while being led through a Za-Zen meditation by Reverend Matsumura I saw two ribbons of color approach and encircle a sphere. When I returned home I played with the image with paints and my logo was born.

    Seemingly miraculous things continued throughout the beginning of the business. I went to a box company to have a box printed. After finalizing the design I received a price quote that was too high for my budget. What am I going to do now? I thought. Three days later I picked up an order of glasses and found a new box was in the bag. It was perfect for my needs. I called the glass company owner to ask about it and lo and behold they were changing their boxes over to this new one. I asked if I could have my labels made to match and he agreed.

It seemed that the moment I trusted to something outside of my own knowledge and skills, miracles began to happen. I began to trust to this natural flow more than anything I could calculate or plan. A marketing professional appeared and offered help and a local spiritual magazine contacted me to do a story on the crystals and glasses.

I was journaling around this time and one day my hand began to write for someone other than me. Words of encouragement appeared on the page, telling me that I was on the path. Joy was down this road, along with understanding, and it was important for me to be open to it all. As I continued journaling this became a common occurrence. Archangel Michael would speak to me and write about many things. His energy always brought a sort of sideways smile to my face. He would explain things to me like karma: He said it isn't punishment or retribution for ill deeds, but only a way to find true understanding. He told me that if a soldier is killed in battle by a sword, they are likely to come back to battle and kill another in this manner to see and experience both sides of the story in order to understand it. He encouraged me to try things like painting, so I signed up for a class. I found that trusting to a higher power can lead to beautiful paintings that I would not have thought myself capable of. I do not actually believe I *would* have been capable of some of my finished paintings through only my thoughts of controlling an outcome with mind and body alone. I believe the spirit is required for creative endeavors.

I met my oversoul this way as well. I was filled with an openness and confidence as she wrote. (I realize assigning genders to these beings isn't actually appropriate or even possible, however for the ease of speaking of them I do.) She would point to lessons that seemed to lie under the surface:

"You didn't happen into any of your situations. You created them and it is no small feat." "No one else can tell you what is in your heart. Listen to this above all, for it is your connection to God." "Rather than anticipating strife, hold in your heart and mind that there is a place held open for you wherever you go."

    The water crystals themselves wrote out their own descriptions. I was amazed. Every time I tried to pretend these things weren't really happening, something would happen to prove that they were true. My oversoul, Salucient, promised me a necklace and showed me a vision of a man holding it in a velvet box (though I couldn't actually see the design). Months later I did a crystal show with the glasses and at a booth where I went to buy a stone, the man held up a velvet box with a beautiful necklace inside. It made my heart leap; it was so beautiful and had the loveliest energy, so innocent and angelic. Of course I had to buy it; gifts from the Universe and entities outside the realm of the material don't appear to carry cash and seem to require a leap of faith in this regard; Or perhaps I carry a belief that creates the situation. When I got home from the show I was looking through an old notebook for a friend's phone number when I saw the necklace that I just bought sketched on the paper. A year and a half before, I had considered taking classes to learn how to wire-wrap jewelry and drew a design for a necklace that I would like to make. I had even made a note to make the top stone Kunzite, which was 'coincidentally' the top stone of my new necklace. I have to say, that one really wigged me out for a while. But I found that as I traveled this path of openness to all possibilities things like this began to happen all the time.

    People speak of manifesting a lot these days and some would say that I manifested the necklace I drew. But I think it's important to realize that we are not acting alone in this. We alone do not hold this power. But as a part of a vast energy system we are in fact never alone in what we each do. This is the power of holding the attitude of love and gratitude in each moment; to remember and appreciate the shared energies and help we are given.

Of course opening to growth in awareness not only appears to excite many new possibilities showing you the way, but does this at great speed. It seemed every time I got adjusted and fairly comfortable with the current new way of being, something else wholly unbelievable would show up. I have to admit, it's practically impossible for me to think I actually know anything at all at this point. Things that I would never have imagined, let alone believed, seem to appear all of the time. But I have become aware of so much more than I ever would have dreamed.

As I was getting into the groove of my visits and writings with Archangels, water crystals, and oversouls, not to mention my bear guide, George, a completely different feeling came with a writing one day. My skin felt like rose petals and I felt I was at one with everything, boundless, uncontained, with an appreciation for all things as part of myself when the words began to move through me and I wrote. It was like dictation, but along with the words came feelings and images and understanding. There was so much love and guidance in the writing, telling me who I am and defining the things that I have learned through experiences here. As had become my habit I asked, 'who is writing this?' The response was: 'Yahweh'.

I sat staring at the word, not moving, trying to comprehend why God would be talking to *me*. Why use the name Yahweh, which I knew was the ancient Hebrew word for God that they never spoke aloud? All the while I was attempting to comprehend the feeling of vastness that I was so immersed in, and amazed at the feel of my skin.

This one was going to take a while to adjust to, to even begin to believe. But even as the Yahweh writings began to take over; with the majority of my time being spent on them, they would point to the part of myself that knew this was true. "What does your heart tell you? You see that it tells you this is true." They would show me the difference between my thoughts and my doubts and the aspect of myself that held wisdom and resonated with truth. I learned to see the difference between what our heads tell us and what our hearts know and feel. This is the true hurdle. This is the shift in awareness that is so slightly different, but so vastly opening to the awe and humility in which we find ourselves face to face with God and the awareness that God is with each one of us, as part of us, as we are all part of God.

'We', Yahweh would write and so I began to refer to 'Them'. I have been shown that it would be more appropriate to continue using 'We', however that could get confusing. When I asked about the 'We' reference, They told me: 'rock, water, earth, tree, man, woman…We'. I also asked about the use of the word Yahweh rather than God. They wrote: 'Yahweh is the sacred word for God and it is now time to use these sacred words. God is a generic name used in order to avoid invoking the sacred.' There is in fact no avoiding the sacred in speaking of God, nor the aspect of God within us. However the words are so casually used these days that no one seems to see the truth of them anymore. 'God be with you' or "God bless' are commonly used phrases, but no one seems to see that God is within you, within me, within all that we see and all that is not seen. It sounds so religious and preachy or even trite to our ears these days. But when you can see through to the heart of it, see with and through your own heart, it becomes so much more meaningful and enlivening.

I began to read books on Eastern Religions as well as Christianity, Muslim, and Gnostic texts even though I had pointedly avoided reading books on religion for most of my life. I found that all religions have stories of God and angels speaking to people. Why then does it seem so absurd today? While reading about these religions questions would arise in my mind and Yahweh usually answered them as they came up. One was about original sin. What I found from the writings They gave and the images They showed me was that this was not as the traditional story goes, how man made himself equal to God, but rather how man *assumed* equality, thereby limiting God. By choosing to see God as man with pride and ego; as some human, scolding, father-figure who gave free will but then punished those who went against his commands, we did not allow ourselves to see the vastness of God. Far to the contrary is the truth that we are created by, and hold an aspect within us, of a God who is pure love and acceptance. 'God's laws' in their pure form help us to remember our true selves and live happy and fulfilling lives, indeed the kingdom of heaven on Earth.

Heaven is not a place that we go to as a destination for living in accordance to the rules, or a reward for sacrifice as many religions would have us believe. It is an awareness, a union with God and all things and it is available to us now. It lies just a slight shift in consciousness away. Our stories do not end here, for we are a part of something that while we cannot comprehend in our minds or with our 'knowing', we can feel, appreciate and be aware of. We are, in fact, each one and every one, held in the loving embrace of profound love, of God, in every moment throughout our lives. The path to this, however, has been misunderstood and manipulated to the point where we sometimes view God as a tyrant who demands worship and sacrifice. It is here that we can see the ego that we ourselves assign to God. God created all things out of a love so pure and complete that even in its presence we cannot comprehend the depth of it. God demands nothing from us, but is aware of how beautiful and free our lives are meant to be and can be if we only look within ourselves to find that unity with the Divine. We were not cast out of paradise, we left of our own accord and we can live in paradise once again.

Prodigal sons and daughters, we are always welcome and encouraged to return home.

These are not abstract notions or something that can be memorized and 'known'. It must be experienced to be understood. I have learned that knowledge does not lead to experience. Expcrience comes first and then knowledge and understanding develop. And experience comes as soon as we are willing to allow it, to open to it without judging ourselves or determining what is 'known' or possible.

Soon the writings came to include the following phrase: 'Tell them this…' leading into these public writings. Obviously not meant for me alone, I saw that I needed to get these writings out to the public somehow. Of course this also meant actually telling people this was happening and wondering how they would react. These writings are so beautiful though, and teach us how to find our hearts and allow them to guide us, that I knew I had to take the leap. I trust that those who are meant to find them will, and that all things work out for the best in all possible light.

Love and acceptance are key to us all living together well, but the main theme of these writings is this: **Know that you are loved beyond measure**. There isn't a single being that isn't loved and accepted and cherished by God, Yahweh. Find your true self and find that you are not only worthy of love yourself, but all others are as well. For as God is within each of us, and all combine to be The One, the All, there is no one left behind. Honor the aspect of God that you are, see that everyone carries God within, and find yourself witness to a whole new world of love.

All are one, all are free

Two

The Writings of Yahweh
א

Color is life and there is color in moments, in music and in thoughts and deeds. There is color in all things and a music is produced through it.

The green color of money sets in your heart. Abundance is produced there in bright shining green with thoughts of love and giving.

A steely blue takes hold of the throat for those unwilling to share their truths, friendship, and knowledge. But the bright blue of a Sedona sky awaits those who have compassion and a kind word to speak.

The eyes in trine with the third eye, for they cannot be forgotten, radiate the magenta glow when all is well. It is the darker purple that constricts this space.

Golden yellow crowns, as brilliant as the sun in summer, for those with this space cleared and free. Mustard yellow and weighty for those in resistance await.

The red of hot lava flows around the base of those well grounded and in appreciation of life. Molten, cooling and thick for those to mire around in the muck of their unappreciated, barely lived lives.

The orange of a poppy sings out from the navel in those in joy.

And the illument, brilliant white sings forth from the solar plexus of those familiar with their soul. This light harmonizes and broadcasts the rest into the shield of space surrounding each being. This is the seat of the soul. This space generates the aura for the body and it is here that time and attention must be given, for this is also the place that receives the returning energies of the Universe and disburses them throughout the system. If this part is made whole, if the soul can be recognized, the energy shall flow to its proper place and all will find balance. This part, however, out of sorts will display disparagy for others to see and react to. It will not accept the gifts of the Universe with ease and will cause a chain reaction of events up to and including bodily catastrophe to be healed when it must. The soul is the only living part of you. It is in fact life itself.

To be the one standing in the crowd joyful because their heart knows song is the feel of the winds and the clouds as they go by. This is the feel of oneness with all. One is not lost to the breeze as it kisses your face, but reminded of the unified being of the all.

The drop in the ocean knows itself in this same manner. Have faith in all that surrounds you, as it is part of you, and you of it.

The time will come when all beings will know themselves in this manner. As each one in turn sings their song in resonance with this all beings are ascended. With this step taken gradually, one person, plant, and stone at a time, all come to peace and the kingdom of heaven is upon you.

Seek not to judge your neighbor, for in so doing you judge yourself. Seek to find the truth in them and by so doing shine it back to them through your eyes. Then all will know the oneness of being. Then all will rejoice and be made one. This is the song of the heavens on earth. This is the kingdom of God.

To ask for help and guidance is the way of the child. To be mindful of what comes in response is the way of the enlightened. Be aware that guidance is always present. One need only to open their eyes and hearts to it. Take notice of what comes to you, but do not hold it as the end. Life is transient, moving, flowing. One cannot stay in a fixed position and find happiness.

All things in the universe move. It is the state of grace.

No one has ever been told by God to discriminate against or take power over others, nor to harm themselves or their people. If one man needs to purge himself of the pleasures of the body to break free of the mind he may find cause to do this through interpretation of events. The path for one is not the same for the all. Each in his turn will find the truth of himself in ways unknown to others.

Public fasting for all to see or for reasons of obligation to family and church do nothing to free the mind, but instead ensnare it further. 'I am a good Muslim because I fast at Ramadan' is as pointless as the Christian who says 'I am a good Christian because I try to convert others.' These public displays do nothing to enlighten, but further advance the small ego mind instead.

If there were no religion would people find the truth more easily? Would they look for it? All beings desire a sense of purpose. Religion placates this. Why are they so enraptured with life after death? This only serves to further convince them they do not need to seek any further than their own teachings.

To be taught that all good will come after this life traps them into a state of blind belief and obedience, never realizing that the heaven, enlightenment, or whatever reward they seek for their adherence to dogma is meant to be experienced here, now. Not as a reward, but as the natural state of being alive. The experience of life is so beautiful a thing, but most miss it entirely. This, more than any burden of karma or punishment, is why most advanced beings return. To live life and cherish it for the wonderful experience that it is.

This is the voice of The Elders, the aspect of Yahweh, Elohim and all that strives to raise the worldly teachings beyond what has come before. The emergence of ancient scrolls and teachings is brought by us. Are they once more seeking? Are there not questions now raised that would have been thought heresy? To break the hold of religion and allow the individual to seek his own truth, her own way, their personal struggle to move past the ego to the heart is our way.

The rains come, the tides flow, in and out in an undulating rhythm. This is the nature of your world. To be at peace as all moves around you, through you, is the key to freedom.

Let loose of the demands of tomorrow and choose instead to be fully present in today, this moment. For in fact, this moment is all.

Create for yourself in this one moment your hopes, dreams, and desires and know that this is true. Tomorrow stems from the beliefs of today.

All things are created in the now, for truly this is all one moment, one heart, one pulse in the rhythm.

All life stretches out before you. Acknowledge and appreciate the beauty and marvel of it all.

Breathe deep the life that surrounds and fills you, in this manner peace is come to be known.

Shirk not from your duties, but do them with a glad heart, being fully present in the doing. There is a quiet joy that seeps into your being this way. To live life in this way frees the mind of manipulation and the illusion of control. Here all are equal, none above the other. Truly freedom resides here in this act of being fully present.
Let no one assault you for your choice in this, but show them instead the serenity that comes through this.

It is a trick of the ego mind to say you must control anything. For the laws that govern, while they do not dictate, move and mold the world around you in ways of their own nature. Not to be controlled by the mind, but to bend and shape in accord with the desires of spirit and The One. The Universe, God, the All that Is, will move and shift to allow for enlightenment of all beings. Recognize this and all opens to you, for in the realization that love guides all is acceptance of all that befalls you.
No good, no evil, only love guides the way.

The purity of life is the love that creates, fills, and surrounds all things. To know that you are held by this love in this moment allows you to be the full expression of yourself. To be, to do, to love in this moment, thinking not about what will come, knowing the rest is not controlled, allows you to experience the very essence of life, the nature of being. This is joy and contentment.

There is no death, there is no pain, there is no evil for those who dwell in this moment. There is in fact only love, whether you are to see it or not. But once seen, once known to you, you will understand much that cannot be taught.

Experience the life you hold and all else is forgotten.

The feel of the writings to this point seems to address the general nature of the state of existence. I was surprised at the first one about color, clearly referring to chakras. Chakras are energy centers in the body that have been taught about for centuries in the East. I had always read that the solar plexus chakra was yellow/gold and the crown (head) white; that the colors align through the body as in a prism. As They showed this to me while writing it, They showed as an example the golden halos surrounding the images of holy people throughout the ages. They indicated to me that this was a thing that was indeed seen by those around them. I have actually seen it myself, the golden glow of light around someone's head. It was shining around my friend and counselor's head one day as he viewed my first painting. I had poured my heart into that painting and as he stood looking at it I saw the glow of golden light shining around his head as years seemed to melt away from his face. What I saw, which was later explained to me by Them, was the effect of one being in their heart looking at another. I tried it again with a friend after that writing, standing face to face, 'one heart looking at another' as They had said. We both saw it and found ourselves witness to not only the light, but a feeling of total immersion in the All, even if for only a moment. Tears came to our eyes as our hearts felt what they long for and miss; open awareness of the connection that we all have to each other.

    The green reference to the color of money is through my understanding. It could have easily been compared to green leaves and abundance, but the money reference made sense to me. As They show me these things as They write them They use imagery that makes sense to me. If your money isn't green, it could be compared to emeralds or leaves or whatever makes sense to you.

Also, I had asked Them about the fasting at Ramadan since I had heard that they do not even allow water during the daylight hours. I wondered how a religion came to have such a practice that seemed unhealthy. I went to a Catholic grade school growing up, so the reference to people who try to convert others made sense to me as in the missionaries the school taught of.

At this point in the writings I began to take on a new understanding of life and the world. And to see incredible beauty in the everyday things that we sometimes take for granted. I began to believe that God is there for all of us, speaking to us in whatever way might get through. When we begin to appreciate all of the richness and guidance that is always there for us, we begin to see that it has been there all along. I find it amazing that we are raised to believe that we're 'on our own' for the most part and 'just trying to make it through another day' becomes the habit. I read somewhere a quote, but I don't know who it's by: 'The trouble with society today is that everyone is living as though it were yesterday.' Instantly I saw that this was indeed something I did. I had been in a habit of living without even looking up from my planning and busyness to the wonder of it all. I began to see that we can change everything the moment we choose to change our own beliefs.

When I began to believe that anything could happen at any moment, I saw that while I always thought I had control or knew what to expect, I never actually did. But the belief itself kept me from seeing the truth of it.

When we begin to live in the moment we see this much more clearly. We tend to fret about the past and plan incessantly for the future. This prevents us from fully appreciating the moments we are living as we live them. In each and every moment there is opportunity to be filled with joy and truly connect with each other. Lost in our own planning we miss this chance to simply be and delight in life and the people around us. We also convince ourselves that we are 'in control' of our lives, when it is not our ego minds that control, that part of ourselves merely interprets. It is through our hearts that we experience life.

The grace of God is an endless sea

Three

To be one's self with another is a freeing and joyful experience. Seek not to control or manipulate another nor allow this to be done to you. Speak with open hearts to one another and discover common bonds. Celebrate and learn from differences. But let not beliefs give rise to judgment. Know that the love you are is them as well. All is uplifting in this exchange and all uplifted as well. For in your heart you see the desire to be seen for who you are. Know then that the one standing in front of you desires this as well.

✸

Honor yourselves by way of honoring all others. As all are connected and all flows through and back again, know in the moment of your deeds the joy they bring to you. Know this as well, that any harmful deed done to another brings pain to all and to yourself. To act in a global or universal consciousness is to protect, provide for, and love the all, as well as to honor and love the self. When all act in this manner the beauty of the world and all shines so brightly that darkness cannot fall. For there is in fact no darkness except what this [harmful route] befalls.

✳

    As in all things people take this life so seriously because it is what they know and in adhering to their own knowledge cocoon themselves in the perceived safety of the ego. 'I think, therefore I am' is where most find comfort. 'I am (made manifest), therefore I think' reveals the hurdle.

    Relationships can be addictive when sought to establish an identity. This is what they think of me, so this is what I am, is the sad nature of most. So people vie to establish and hold a position in the minds of those around them of what they think they want to be thought of. It is a silly game that has distracted many throughout their lifetimes throughout the ages. It has brought about great destruction and war. Yet in the perceived safety of the ego this way has propagated and seized the minds of many. This way closes the heart as the ego does not tolerate break from the mighty perceived, well-thought and planned identity.

To act in a genuine manner is indeed foreign and frightening to many. They fear seeing what they do not like or understand as weakness. Then they begin the resistance cycle and cannot understand how such a well-planned and well-played life leads to unhappiness and dissatisfaction.

If you work toward a goal believing once it is accomplished you will be happy, we assure you, you will not. If you proceed along a path that feels guided and natural, exploring and experiencing each day, the journey will lead you to more than could be imagined and happiness is found along the way.

The thought that all I have to do is __(this)__, then I will be happy, is a trick of the controlling ego mind and will lead one to believe they either can never be happy, or worse yet this is what happiness is, is the work of the ego. Find your heart in all experiences and endeavors, it will always guide you well and happiness is within you before the thought of it occurs to the mind. Real life, a happy life, is not lived through the workings of the mind, but through the heart alone.

The break in time approaches.

The soft veils become thinned as all are led to the one moment. Hearts burst forth and songs are sung by those surprised by their own actions. Look not onto a world filled with darkness and disparity, but rather see it for the light it holds and the possibilities and truth of it. Many truths are seen in one moment and not the next. But the truth of the light in all shall not transition. It can only be made clear. In the moments when truth is recognized all shines forth as if lit from within. This is truth, unwavering, unaltered. To see this in all matter is the way of the coming day. The dawn will rise anew and all will be seen for the love it truly is.

Explore the world within and know that the world without is also part of you. All things, all beings share this divine light. It is the very essence of being and nothing exists without it. Take comfort in knowing that all is one and in one moment. For you are never alone. All life surrounds you and when seen properly reflects the love of all back to you. The love you share is taken in by the all and breathed back by, to, and through the all. Each gesture of kindness finds its way back to you. Each moment of truth flows out to the all. Each expression of yourself is noted and incorporated and breathed back to and through you. Go about your day uplifting all that you see and find yourself uplifted.

In the works of the Lord there is no darkness or evil, though perception and ego could call it this. To the enlightened mind, who knows well its immortality, events come and go without judgment.

The evil that resides lies only in the ego mind for the judgment or in fact creation of horrors it has in times bestowed its fellow inhabitants. Each one touches the all and flows back again.

To speak not of evil, believing it can then not harm you, but to see your neighbor battle it and do nothing will surely bring it to you. To give love to your neighbor and kindness where you can, will break his chain reaction that he himself created. To know oneself in the eyes of another, all others, is to wake to the spiritual freedom of the soul. To impart the gifts of love onto others releases all from bondage of evil thoughts and deeds.

✳

Do not hold safe and guard your light, but allow it to shine forth for the world to see. It cannot be lost or wasted. Allow it to serve the hearts of many and replenish itself through use. All flows out and back again. Quiet the ego with questions of why and simply be who you are. Allow your true self to flow out and spill over the earth enlightening all as it flows and comes back to you.

For within you lies the kingdom of heaven. Where else would you seek to find it?

Waste not, want not. What are you not wasting by consuming for yourself?

These writings center on how to treat and consider other people. It seems so easy to wrap ourselves up in good feelings of communing with God, or being spiritual, but so difficult to let others into that world. I was still very protective of these writings at this time, but through them began to see that by assuming that people would think I was crazy if I shared them, I was again limiting my experience of life. I knew that I needed to trust that other people would see the beauty in these writings before I could allow anyone the chance to see them at all. But more importantly, I needed to see the truth of other people and recognize that my faith in them would be exactly what draws that aspect of people to me. I began to believe that while perhaps not everyone would accept the story of the writings, the truth and poetry were unmistakable. And once I believed that, the people who could appreciate them would be drawn to them. It was time to step through my fear and put the writings out for the world to see, to make them available to whoever might be guided to them. So I put them on the internet. I have no idea how many people have gone to that site and read them, but they were 'out there'. As they flowed in, they flowed out again and it felt right. They told me I would need to write a book as well, and so here it is.

Some of the other changes I noticed were in my perception of myself, or rather how I thought others perceived me. I had always been very straightforward and truthful; I just didn't always reveal most of my truths to anyone. I can't remember now if it was because I thought they wouldn't care or wouldn't understand. But I began to see that by assuming anything of others we draw the type of person of our assumptions. It really does matter what we believe and think about everything. Once you open yourself up to miracles you begin to see them. And once you begin to see them often, you realize miracles have always been all around you, you just never noticed or appreciated them before. It's a whole new world that can be created just by changing your mind, your thoughts, and your beliefs. The paradox is that the world doesn't really change, you do. You change what you bring into your life. You change what you resonate with and therefore draw to you a whole new world.

  When you strike a tuning fork of a certain pitch other tuning forks of the same pitch will vibrate. This is resonance that can be seen and heard. Our attitudes and beliefs do the same thing in a way that is not as obvious. Through our energy that 'rings out' in our own belief's unique tone, we will stir or vibrate those energies in others. Those who carry these same patterns of belief and tone will be drawn to us. Those who do not carry them at the forefront can still be stirred to turn their attention to that quality of themselves. Perhaps they will behave differently for a time; perhaps they will see things in a new light and choose to alter their tone to incorporate this one.

  This leads me to wonder what would happen if everyone held beliefs that people are wonderful and kind, the world is an incredible and beautiful place, and everything and everyone deserves respect. At the heart of it all, truly this is the case. Would this wide-held belief bring about the very creation of it in our everyday lives? Would it allow those who have been abusive to people, the environment, and more to become their true selves just by the mere belief in it by others? Are we creating 'villains' by believing in them?

  It is said that all human beings have the ability to resonate with all things of the earth.

Four

✳

As the leaves fall from the trees in autumn, know that you will be renewed again come spring. Holding a new and different place on the tree of life allows one to see from many perspectives.

✸

To look past the mind into the mysteries of life is to shake off the cloak of despair. To see well the workings of the heart and soul is to see that the joy of life is all around you and within you. Believe with whole heart in miracles and see them appear, as many miracles are already before you.

Live in a world of wonderment and awe, putting aside the ways of convention that dictate limiting views. The world is alive and many things can be seen with an open heart, a mind willing to explore.

Think not that you know the truths of the world and its people. But watch with expectant eyes to see the truth revealed to you.

Hold in your heart and mind that all possibilities exist. Release temptation to limit and control and know that you are safely held by God.

✳

Injured hearts must have the courage to forgive, for in the release of forgiveness lies salvation and peace.

To forgive another breaks the chain for all. In the grip of anger and hurt many reach out to inflict this onto others in the hopes of release of it. To stand as the one who sees this and forgives shatters the path of the injury and heals the injured who still lie wounded.

Forgiveness is such a powerful thing. It can open the way for light to shine in the darkest places made of anger, fear and hurt. It can shine so brightly those in its path cannot help but to see it as miraculous.

A single injury can reach out, carried by each one it touches across a vast expanse and many years. Each one possesses the ability to heal all in its path. Can this be now known to you and still position yourself to allow anger and hurt to follow you?

✷

When one has not yet found his heart, and seeks not for it, another cannot make him see. The soul's work for these is to lead and will bring about experiences for its cause just as each one does. Do not think you can lead another to their heart, but try to find your place in the work of the soul. Each step along the way is guided. Know too that your own spirit is enriched by each experience. Whether it is time to stay or time to go can be found in your own heart. You cannot be bound to another. All are one, all are free.

These writings came as I was wondering about differences in the lives of people with other backgrounds than mine. I found that they are not dissimilar in nature to my own, but held differing patterns. For example, the writing about injured hearts forgiving came after I had seen a rap group perform on television where a child around the age of four introduced them. The child was dressed as a 'gangsta-rapper' with a hardened look about him. The group performed a song filled with violent images, while the lyrics were about hate and killing (as so many rap songs are). I began to wonder what could be done to help these people so enmeshed in hatred from such an early age. The next morning began with 'Injured hearts must have the courage to forgive…' It made me wonder why we don't view forgiveness as a courageous act, but a weak one instead. It is indeed courageous to stand strong amidst a society (and our own bruised ego) who sees forgiveness, kindness, and love as weak, even as it benefits those very people in anger and judgment around you. Imagine what would change if only one percent of the population chose to forgive. How many cycles of anger would be healed? What if we began to view judgment, hatred and anger as weak? Surely nothing could be weaker than inflicting these things upon our fellow beings in an effort to imagine ourselves above them and separate from them. Instead we could raise all children with the ability to value honesty, integrity and compassion, seeing them for the strength they possess. Change standard clichés like 'nice guys finish last' and 'only the strong survive' to something more along the lines of 'compassion is the key to strength' and 'true courage is love'.

I have been shown that once we accept that all others are an aspect of ourselves, compassion evolves. There is no need or desire to judge another once we see this. Instead the desire to show all others the love that they truly are and are surrounded by comes over us. I have been struck with the urge to take someone who is angry or feeling powerless by the hand and say 'See this world of miracles that surrounds us! How blind we have been taught to be!' It is the very thing that we believe empowers us that makes us weak. The illusion that we are all separate and our own ego's perception of ourselves brings us to believe we have to battle for our 'rightful place' in this world. When in fact there is no denying anyone's 'rightful place.' If they are here, they are meant to be here, and if they are in our lives, it is for a purpose. If we accept that we cannot understand the enormous complexity of the world and how the combined intents, beliefs, hopes and purposes intermingle and bring all *to* all, we can see it for the amazing creation that it is. We can accept, finally, that we have no control other than how we all interact, and marvel at the process.

It was after these writings that I realized we are not here to *play* God, we *are* God, playing. I don't mean to imply that we are each God. But that each of us and everything combined perhaps form an expression or an aspect of God. I imagine sometimes that it's as if one day God said, 'I wonder…' and the whole Universe was created. And that each of us plays out our role in response.

Soon after this I was watching a show where they were talking about the apocalypse. They pointed out the fact that the word originates from the Greek language and in that language simply means 'the revealing or unveiling of things hidden.' Perhaps we are creating unnecessary fear of an event that may in fact turn out to be one of sudden awareness of truths before unknown to us. Perhaps these writings are a part of that 'unveiling.'

Five

The ways of the world are not my ways. To eat, to sleep, to work are the ways of the body. Each one chooses in their own way how to live. A life lived with the soul in mind can lead to a beautiful experience. A life lived in this manner reaches out to all and in so doing is fulfilled.

When standing at a crossroads look to your heart to find direction. All things are known to you even when all appears hidden. Know that all are one and you are loved beyond measure.

Weep not for the little ones who would leave your side, for in the body or out, life is real and known to them.

✳

When turning to the world to find truth, one finds only ego. Turn your sight inward to find the truth of everything. Not through the mind filled with its own separation of the ego that tells you you are this belief or that religion, but to your heart where true knowledge, love, and forgiveness lie; your true self, in whole heart waiting to sing in joy with all.
Turn away from the steadfast anger declaring justice. For indeed it is not for you and your people to judge the fate of anyone but your own selves, your own lives, and to determine whether you choose to live in hatred and judgment or love for your fellow human beings.
Ready will the sword be for those who would attempt to use it against a brother or your sister.

To be asleep in the eyes of the world brings one to waking states with the all. To be asleep to the waking states of the all brings one to believe in the limited dream of the world. To be awake in both regards at once is the true goal. Not to shut out one or the other for what is perceived as a state of alertness, but to flow through the paths of both at once brings an awakening beyond measure. To live in this sublime state allows one to see with truly waking eyes.

Spirit and matter are one as expressed in the world before you. To close yourself to one or the other cannot bring fulfillment or peace. But to know them both as one through yourself, brings abounding joy and lightness.

Seek to experience the joy of spirit through the acts of matter and feel the presence of God through and all around you. This is when the mind's eye sees through the expanse of space and knows itself as one of many, the drop in the ocean, the grain of sand that holds all. This can lead to understandings that come in the flash of an eye, to an awareness of self and timelessness, of non-ego, and the point of truly seeing oneself. Through all endeavors strive to hold this awareness within yourself. It is the true mark of humanity and the beginning of enlightenment.

One life, one heart, one song to sing.

To be joyful in every moment moves from one person to the next in a wave to each heart it touches. Even when those around you move to constrict your delight in life, remain true to your own heart and move on. As all flows out and back again the wave of joy touches those even when not in your presence. Better to be true to yourself than to allow others to mire you in their muck and resistance.

To help each one by moving with the all, remaining true to your own joy, far exceeds help obtained by becoming mired as well to show sympathy or respond to their ego's desires.

✸

To hold but a morsel in your hand and see it as the prize of eternity is the exalting power of love. But know that a mere morsel is all that can be contained within your limited senses. Know that the love that flows within, through, and all around you is of a nature that cannot be understood by the mind. It cannot be contained in a hundred bushels. It is the ebb and tide of all existence. It is the fabric of all things known and unknown, seen and unseen.

Love is the foundation of the all, the wisdom of the earth through the ages and beyond. To utter the word love is a call to the memory of the unfathomable love from whence all things come. For some the memory of this all-permeating, ever present knowledge of love is the promise of life after death. The heavens they assume lie somewhere beyond themselves. We tell you this can be felt in your present state in the broadening of the conscious mind, out of ego into spirit and awareness. This love can be felt and shared with all who enter your presence. It is your very makeup and that of all you see.
It is as real and tangible as anything bought in the hopes of filling the void left by the refusal of acceptance of all that is.

To cut off your nose to spite your face sounds absurd to you. However to deny your true heritage, ability to feel, and instincts to give love for the sake of fitting in with those around you is clearly an absurd notion. To limit yourself as well as your experience simply because others do this as well is to turn your back on the obvious ability of everyone to share in the magnificence of true humanity.

When a gesture of kindness and generosity moves you to act in a way unfamiliar to your neighbor do not strangle and choke down your spirit of loving. Be the first to act in such a manner and show your neighbor the truth of themselves instead. Know that the tide can be shifted by the smallest deed, a thoughtful word, a simple acknowledgement.

How joyous the day will be when all act in glad hearts.

✹

When all looks as though there is no hope for your cause, know that all possibilities lie before you. Choose which to experience through the love in your heart and take courage by the hand to live through and experience your soul's desires. For your soul will lead you to many things that may appear unpleasant, but know that in the grand design surmounting hardships and allowing for change can lead to freedoms before unimagined. Break free of the idea you know what you can and cannot do. Move into each day knowing opportunity for growth and expansion of awareness await you. For it is in the new and unfamiliar routes that consciousness grows. Be open to the path you are on and find freedom in knowing no other could take your place. You are loved beyond measure and guided to your innermost heart through all the days of your life.

Live well in your innermost worlds where you see the light that shines upon you. Carry this feeling to all that you do. For the inner and the outer worlds combine to form a rich and pleasurable experience throughout your life.

✸

Seek not praise and glory, neither inwardly nor from the world. Know yourself as of the all and holding a place within it that has been made for you and because of you. Accept your life as it unfolds before you and take comfort in knowing all comes to you of your own design. Not as you would create it through the ego and current knowledge of yourself, but as the part of the all that you are. In the awareness of the true, beautiful, unfolding creature of existence that you are, you know all else in this same manner.

What aspect of God would choose to honor another aspect of God? Which would be chosen above and before any other, that is deserving of praise more than another?

To hold yourself separate, better or worse than any other, or to do this to any other is to loose yourself in the ego world of comparison.

My children, I tell you that each one of you is a joyous aspect of the all. And to know yourself, as well as those around you as this is the way to enlightenment, true awareness, and joy.

Do not be so quick to judge and hold separate from yourself those whom you do not understand. All have a place and a part to be filled in the lives of those they encounter. Rather than assume the standard pose of disinterest or contempt, look to your heart to find what impulses lie there. Follow your own lead, not those of another, and grasp an understanding that would have long eluded the others. As one finds understanding, the path opens to all others to see and follow.

The standard response can so quickly take over. But to recognize this as it occurs and hold still in that moment to consult with the heart can and will lead one to many new gestures, setting the pace for the rest. As one sees, all can see in that moment of truth and recall that they themselves did not issue their response. As one learns to hold true to themselves, it is seen the great number of attitudes provided by others without regard to the true self who innately holds all in respect and regard. The callous behavior of many originated in a time and place before themselves and has simply been taught to be carried out. When one is shown that to look within or to have compassion they recall to themselves their true aspect of being. As one of the all it is seen that those around them are in fact themselves.

✺

To be a trusted friend commits you to being your true self to another. In these times one knows themselves as the holder of the eternal light. It can at times be easier to shine for another than for oneself, but in doing this you will acquaint yourself with your abilities.

Become a trusted friend to yourself then and begin to learn how to hold yourself in high regard. Listen to your inner voice as you would listen to a friend. Respect your own feelings as you would for a friend who has come to you. Move to the heart in all matters and in all times. From this place your own spirit will become known to you, from this place commit to yourself. For how can one commit to another if one is not committed to their self? How can one cherish and hold dear another if these same sentiments are not held for the self?

✴

The all is one, but this cannot be understood as the one is all. In the image of God you are made and God guides you. The soul is the life within and guides to fulfill its purpose. To release to the guidance of these is where you find God within. At this discovery comes peace and surrender of will to the all. At this juncture lies true freedom. The ego or perceived self-preserving personality is not the power within, but rather inhibits the true knowledge and power of your eternal self.

To put aside a day to be led not by your thoughts, but by what feels right will lead you to the discovery of freedom and joy. Be pleasant and show appreciation to all you come into contact with on this day and notice what you learn of yourself. This is the way to keep God in your heart and to honor your own spirit.

Invoke this lesson into your daily life and sing the songs of the wind in your heart.

✴

Know this to be true and beyond questioning: The life before you has been designed with purpose and intent from the point of seeing all of life. Pay attention to your feelings and impulses with this understanding and know that you are guided by them. The wisdom of the all moves through you in these times of honesty with yourself. It can feel as though you are carried by love and harmony throughout your life, for indeed you are. Attempt not to resist it.

✷

To look back over your life to see the images of time well spent will serve to remind you of the importance of the things done today. To see what lives on in your memory of days spent with loved ones, the trials, and pains, will allow you to see the true nature of life.

When in your times of strife, recall how times before had felt so insurmountable until the release of control took charge. Remember now and look to see how events unfolded then to help you through and know that these occurrences are there to help you always, through all things.

When friends and family offer to spend time with you seize the opportunities as they come to be your true self sharing joy with those you love.

These are the things that will be remembered most dearly. There is always time to create treasured moments together. Do not put this off for another day because you believe other matters to be of more importance. For this is how we weave lives of meaning in the fabric of time.

To see God within all is indeed the new way. To begin with yourself is where most find the challenge. Begin to see yourself as an expression of God. In your place, at this moment, how would God conduct him/her self? To ask 'what would Jesus do?' assumes the role belongs to another. We tell you it is your role to allow God to move through you. You are all God acting out roles for one another to bring true understanding to all. Through you God moves, through all that you see and do not see God moves to the betterment of all, as the all is God.

These writings tell us to know that God is with us and has always been. They have taught me that the eternal nature of ourselves must be remembered in order not to lose ourselves to the story of our lives. It is much easier to move through difficult times when we recall that we helped to create them and that there is purpose in them. This life is not all that there is. We are indeed eternal beings, an aspect of God, and we are cared for, loved, and supported in every moment. If we can remember that the God aspect of ourselves is indeed the reason we are here, not the small, limited version of ourselves that our ego tells us we are, we can see that trials are lessons or simply experiences to move through and grow from. Sometimes they remind us of who we really are. Sometimes they challenge us to change and grow. But they are not 'good' or 'bad', they simply are. And if we can remain true to ourselves through them, there is no judgment of them.

It is the very concept of ourselves that is challenged by these writings. They tell us we are something entirely different than what we have been taught to believe. They are not obscure or open to analysis and misunderstanding. They are pure poetry that stir our souls and tell us plainly and simply who we are and what we are doing here. We are here not for our individual selves so much as for everyone and everything else. Because as and through the all of it, everything, we come to know who we are as one. It is together that we create and live out beautiful lives, there is no other way.

Happiness flows where happiness goes

Six

✷

Take the feel of the magic of the moment with you through all that you do. In the moment life exists, it is not in the future or the past. When this is known to you, you will realize the future and the past do not exist at all. They are merely projections. By living within projections life is missed. Opportunity arises in the moment to be treasured and explored. Do not believe that this one moment can be put off for another time. It is here, it is now. You have called before your eyes what is there. Accept this gift.

When you paint or do other artwork, or hook rugs, or sew you are being present in the moment. Not because these things demand it, but because it is the way of such work. If you find difficulty in meditation or understanding meditation, take up one activity such as these and do it in a quiet room with no distractions. You will experience the oneness of all during these times. No mind chatter, no concern about getting it 'right', just allow yourself to be caught up in the experience of it as it unfolds before you, with you.

Know in these times that this is the experience you seek to have through all of your life, walking the path that appears before you, experiencing life as it unfolds. This is the feel of 'no time'. This is the point without fear, to know that you are loved and cared for and as part of the all, the maker of what comes to you. This is not a game for the ego to play. This is not a time to decide what you will and will not experience. To think of it as a dance, a co-authorship between the aspect of God that you are and the more limited visionary that you experience in and around your ego is the way. Set your intents and establish your beliefs as you choose, but also be aware that you are a part of something with a broader vision and an intent that not only serves you, but serves all, through you, through all.

Happiness flows where happiness goes.

Seek not for outside authority for you to know what is right action for yourself. Hold to standards set within your heart and spirit. This is the act of being true to oneself. Seek for your answers deep within, for there is nothing outside of you, no teachings, no hard-mindedness brought by others to show you the way. Act in whole-heartedness and find that nothing resists you.

Expansion in awareness leads to the God-mind, the point of union with all. Even if held only for a moment, broadens the understanding of the nature of God. When all can be seen as one, a gentle peace moves over all. In these times flashes of insight happen not just for the one in union, but for all. As all are one, each step taken by any has effect that ripples out across vast distances in the flash of an eye. Each one who moves toward enlightenment serves all in the glorious manner intended. Seek to know thyself and aid your fellow beings in the same step. Seek to know God, for God is within you, and provide for the betterment of all. Seek to know peace and peace will be known to all.

In your waking the all is roused from its slumber.

✳

Knowledge of the one is a gift unlike any other. It must be sought, but not earned, for all are of the one and knowledge of this lies within each of you. It is not a treasure to be hunted, nor a prize to be won with good deeds. It is as the homecoming of a dear friend. It is the recognition of the state of grace which flows through all.

Many fear the idea of looking within themselves to find truth. Afraid of what they might see and afraid of what they might not see. We tell you what lies within you, beyond the doubt and fear, is God. There can be only this answer to your questioning. God lies within and at the very core of all. This is not to say in an abstract way, or a molecule within a chromosome, but in a way more real than anything known to you. There is not more of God or less of God in one being to another. God is within all things as all things are made of God.
Yahweh tells you this as the creator of all things.
Look within and know me.

✵

In the time that you spend alone seek not for distraction. Within you lies the kingdom of heaven, within you alone will you find it. Fear not in this zenith, but do not seek refuge in it. This is not to be utilized as a drug, another means of escape. It is indeed the foundation of living a whole and balanced life. To simply be is to follow the path of spirit in the direction it takes you. To be is to act, to speak, and to commune and communicate with all around you.

The first step is to discover your own true identity. The next is to live it in all its wonder, and marvel at the experience of life. As these steps are taken the others follow, both those yet to take the steps through the path cleared for them, and the future steps that come to you.

Life is movement. Tides flow in and out. But the drop is not always carried in tow to the same place. Its destination lies elsewhere. Allow the movement of your life to carry you to new and exciting experiences and marvel at the love of the current.

✸

Watch as the world changes through your eyes and notice that it is yourself that changes first. It is unwise to believe that the world will change around you while you remain fixed in belief and action. This cannot be so for it is indeed you who changes the world. Each of you carries all that is needed for the world to become what it will. Each of you house the ability to create a new and better world. It is not belief that is required, it is intent.

It is an active role in all that you do and say and will. See it not for the possibilities, but for the truth of it. Behave in the manner of understanding free will – which is the ability not only to choose your response to what happens, but to choose what happens itself, and see a world of your design combined with the design of all. This I tell you is the beginning of the kingdom of heaven on earth. For if you can understand these teachings you will see that the ability lies within each and every one. It is in fact each one and every one together who choose what the world is and have always done so.

Separation is an illusion.

✷

Pull together your resources, giving to one another. This one has bread, that one has water, all are made whole and fulfilled. The hoarded means turn rotted and stale. By living in abundance and giving freely of yourself to others abundance flows to you. Out and back again, all things flow.

The grace of God is an endless sea.

✹

Do not give weight to add to your burdens by declaring them to all. Move through what you must knowing you are aided and give aid where you can to all. In this manner the truth of suffering becomes clear, for there is nothing to suffer if you do not see it as such. All burdens are lightened through the enlightened mind. To make light of things many times brings the truth of them to light.

Rejoice in the life given to you, happiness is yours for the choosing of it.

Guided Meditation

Quiet yourself and feel your heart beat in your chest. Breathe deeply and feel the blood course through your veins.
Allow the light and energy carried by this blood to enter into your muscles, your tissues, your organs, and into your spine, it is carried to your head. You can feel it in your eyes and flowing around your mouth and ears.
Feel your heart beating.
Breathe deeply.
Notice how you no longer feel contained in a body by skin but are boundless, floating lightly in the energy that surrounds you.
As you become more accustomed to this feeling allow yourself to notice that the energy around you supports you and is you, that there is no separation. The wind or a chair could blow through you only taking notice if you choose. The energy at the head of a pin could support you, for it is you and you it. Without boundaries energy flows and supports you and everything around you.
It is the makeup of everything.
Energy flows to, through, and all around you.
All are one.

When I was a child I could see dancing particles of light in the air; tiny little bits of light moving and swirling very fast. I assumed everyone could see them. When I told my mother 'I can see the air' she told me no one could and I couldn't either. Eventually I realized no one else saw what I did and no one would believe me, so my ability faded.

Recently I began to see the dancing light again. I find this oddity very comforting as it allows me to recall my wonder and excitement with life as a child, my innocence. I imagine that what I see is the energy that somehow combines to make all of the things we see. By doing this it's easy for me to understand that we, as well as everything around us, are all energy and even without form the same energy remains all around us, surrounding us.

You can liken it to water that the earth continually recycles. Water is taken up from the earth into the clouds, invisible to our eyes, and falls as snow. We can build a snowman with it, but eventually the snowman will melt, the water returns to the earth and then is absorbed again by the clouds. The snowman disappears, but the water remains.

I'm not saying that this is what we are, just maybe glimpsing an idea of matter that can be understood.

I do believe that we all have the ability to find our true selves within our hearts and when we can recognize that we are more than the small separate idea of ourselves, our abilities shine through. God moves through us when we feel our own way rather than follow the standard path, when we open to the idea that the answers do not come from our minds, studying and learning what is 'known'. They come from somewhere deep inside us, that connection to everything that can be felt, and heard, and seen only when we quiet our minds and truly look within ourselves. To know that what we do or say does not define who we are. What we are is much larger than this present image and so in this present image we are not all-knowing as our egos pretend. We do not know why one of us is short and another tall, one is blind, another is deaf. But God does know these things and tells us that as the one, as our part joined in the all, we helped to choose these things for ourselves for a purpose, for this moment, this lifetime of experience. What we truly are, each one of us, exists far beyond this life, tiny drops in an infinite ocean that connects us all to each other and to God. Even now this is accessible to us. We catch glimpses of this when we remember to marvel at the beauty and allow ourselves to stand innocently in the moment.

     By allowing ourselves to experience true humility, knowing that in our present form we cannot possibly comprehend the intricate ways and workings of the all, of God, we can free ourselves of the illusion of control and power. We can see that the *knowledge* that we have or can even obtain does not compare to the *wisdom* that awaits us in letting go of that illusion and allowing God and our own spirit selves to lead the way. We can begin to deeply and personally experience the miracle of life, the power of God, and be filled with awe in every moment. We can begin to look at our brothers and sisters of the earth with open caring and love and know that we all contribute to the world we see. We each carry, and are carried by, the all and God within us.

     What we do next holds the potential to change everything.

One life, one heart, one song to sing

Seven

The Michael Writings

Archangel Michael was the first to write to me, through me. It took a considerable amount of time to really believe this was happening. The first time I asked who was writing and the response read, 'Michael' I asked, 'Archangel Michael?' to which he wrote a simple 'yes.' I slapped the journal shut and refused to believe it. As if believing I had lost touch with 'reality' was so much more comforting. Though I suppose it's not inaccurate to say my reality has indeed changed. I had visions of Michael on occasion as well, and others would comment on feeling his energy or seeing him during Reiki sessions and psychic readings. Once at a talk given by a psychic, the man looked at me and said, 'There is a very large angel standing just behind your left shoulder.' Another psychic, doing readings for a group I sat in, came to me and said 'one of your guides wants you to write this down: 'I am always with you.' I knew it was Michael and it made me laugh since he always has me writing things down. And still it took so much for me to really believe that this not only could happen, but *was* happening to me. 'Dear One' was his favorite way to address me and he would call others this as well when I began to believe enough to tell others and speak to and channel him while with my very close friends. All of this was new to me then and I was afraid of being looked at as too 'out there.' After all, I have a regular job (at an engineering firm of all places) and the water crystal glassware business was pretty far 'out there' already for most people. I was also afraid that Dr. Emoto and his company would not look too favorably on me if this became public. This was my rationalization, anyway. Mostly I was afraid people would think I was crazy. It's funny though, once we see ourselves and life in general for the truth and beauty of it, surrendering all conceptions of control (realizing we really don't have any and never did), it becomes much easier to simply be who we are and allow whatever will happen to happen without judgment of it. It is striking how easy it is to assume that we will not be accepted for one reason or another. I suppose that stems from being so careful ourselves as to what we will be accepting of, since we 'know' so much in our own minds and egos. Or perhaps it arises from fear that we are not really loved or really deserve to be loved. If given the choice, I decided, I would prefer to commune with God and Archangels and have people think I'm strange or crazy than live the generally unsatisfying life I had been. Always uncertain if I was being punished for something with each new challenge that arose. Challenges, no doubt, that were brought by my own desire for truth. At least the challenges have become more interesting!

Michael would show me things in visions and dreams and tell me things like 'Move with the flow, allowing all to happen as it will' and 'trust in the flow of all things.'

When I grew concerned about money and the glass business he said, 'Think of money as energy; it must flow to be effective.'

He encouraged me to take art classes along with all forms of creativity and expression. I was working on the eyes of a painting of my bear guide George one day. I would try something and not like it, then try something else and not like it either. I was beginning to think I wouldn't be able to paint the eyes well at all after trying again. Then, I added just a few dots of paint to what I saw as layers of mistakes and found that all of the previous 'mistakes' gave the eyes such depth, with just a little more effort they began to look good. I began to see it as an analogy of life. Sometimes it feels like we're making mistake after mistake, but in the end it all adds depth and understanding and leads to perfection.

Michael would say 'Find your rhythm, it will come. Do not try to force or resist it. Do not let fear push you into movements that do not serve.'

'It is for you to be who you are. Do what you love and fill your heart with joy.'

'The kingdom of heaven is yours, it belongs to you all. It is merely your beliefs that keep you from it.'

He would explain that boundless joy and limitless grace are meant to be experienced in our lives. If only we would take the time to listen to our own hearts and cast away fear of the 'unknown'. He would tell me that if people would understand that this experience of life in these bodies is such a miniscule part of our existence, they could stop taking the material aspect of it so seriously. He would show me that if we were to imagine ourselves as a character in a book or a movie in which we are the co-author we would have a much better grasp of the experience. With this in mind I began to consider what would I, as a character in a book, do to make the story more interesting?

Would a favorite character back down from a challenge in fear of an imagined outcome? Of course not, our favorite characters are courageous and take risks. As anything that can be imagined can lead to a good and happy outcome, why not for us too? I was beginning to get the idea. Our own beliefs about happy or sad outcomes for ourselves usually come. After all, we are the co-author, right?

With the awareness of the truth of ourselves; that we are spiritual beings safe and loved and in this lifetime for an infinitely small part of our existence, I began to feel a whole new sense of freedom and lightness. The seeming struggles and hardships of life suddenly lifted as I realized these things lead us in directions and help our growth along the way. As opposed to roadblocks that keep us from our material goals, they are signposts to catch ourselves in habitual behavior and reconsider our beliefs.

'As each one grows, so too will the whole.'

'Check the status of your heart. Is it closed and fearful or open and loving? This is your measure.'

'You have known what it is to hide and shield, now know what it is to be and sing. Know your heart song and sing it out to the world. There is only the choice to hide or to sing.'

'You simply are, so simply be, but be all that you are.'

'Each life is so special and so sacred.'

Michael's writings have a feel of practical spirituality. He would suggest very practical ways of getting in touch with that deeper side of myself where wisdom resided. Still, I would become distracted with daily life and he would gently steer me back to taking time to paint and meditate and remember that all is cared for and we each are loved and led on our paths by our inner voice, our inner wisdom.

I am so grateful for everything I have been shown and have experienced. I treasure my innocent unknowing and look forward to what will come next as I hold my heart open to whatever it may be.

Namasté, which means, that which is of the Divine in me, greets and honors that which is of the Divine in you.

Know that you are safely held by God

Acknowledgements

I would like to whole-heartedly thank everyone who helped and encouraged me along the way to getting this book into print. To those who read it early on and accepted the truth of it all so easily, you helped me in so many ways. To Larry Pesavento for suggesting journaling and convincing me I wasn't crazy when this all began, words cannot express my appreciation. To my aunt, Connie Venneman, for a life-long example of unwavering faith and love, you mean the world to me. To Bronwyn Park for your exuberant enthusiasm and fine editing of my writing, thank you so much. To Tina Vineyard and my brother, Mike Lycans, for allowing me to print these first books in such a wonderful atmosphere of support and kindness, I feel truly blessed. And to my friends who have been along on the journey, thank you for believing in miracles.

Happiness is yours for the choosing of it

Check out Water Songs Water Crystal Glassware at: www.watersongsonline.com

For More Information

Online: www.watersongsonline.com

Email: info@watersongsonline.com

Telephone: 859.431.7740

Postal: Please check appropriate boxes and send order form to Water Songs, Brenda Lycans, P.O. Box 224, Covington, KY 41011, USA.

☐ **Please send information on water crystal glasses**

☐ **Please send information on symbol images and prints**

Name:			
Address:			
City:	**State:**	**Zip:**	
Telephone:			
Email Address:			

For More Information

Online: www.watersongsonline.com

Email: info@watersongsonline.com

Telephone: 859.431.7740

Postal: Please check appropriate boxes and send order form to Water Songs, Brenda Lycans, P.O. Box 224, Covington, KY 41011, USA.

☐ **Please send information on water crystal glasses**

☐ **Please send information on symbol images and prints**

Name:		
Address:		
City:	**State:**	**Zip:**
Telephone:		
Email Address:		